S0-CIH-173

The Life of Mary

Written by Carol Ann Morrow

Illustrated by Ave O. Macasiray

ISBN 1-936020-14-0

Mary is born to Joachim and Anna. We celebrate her birthday on September 8th. Decorate this cake in honor of Mary's birthday.

Mary's parents take her to the Temple to thank God for their beautiful daughter.

Anna and little Mary walk to the well in Nazareth to get water for washing and cooking.

Joachim, Anna, and Mary celebrate the Sabbath. They light the candles on their table.

Her parents teach Mary how to pray the Psalms. Later Mary will pray with her own Child.

Joachim and Anna sometimes travel to the hills to visit their relatives. Mary enjoys a visit with her older cousin Elizabeth, already married to Zechariah.

Joachim and Anna see that their daughter is growing up. It is up to them to choose a good husband for her. They choose a man named Joseph.

When Mary is praying, the angel Gabriel angel comes to see her.
She is very surprised.

Gabriel asks Mary if she is willing to become the mother of the Son of God. Mary asks how this can be, since she has no husband.

The angel tells Mary that God can do impossible things. Mary believes this and says Yes to becoming the mother of Jesus.

Mary asks her parents if she can go to visit her cousin Elizabeth. The angel had told her that Elizabeth is also going to have a baby boy.

Elizabeth is very glad to see Mary. The Holy Spirit reveals to her Mary's surprising news.

Back in Nazareth, an angel tells Joseph about Mary's baby. When Mary returns to Nazareth, she and Joseph get married.

Joseph and Mary must travel to Bethlehem to be counted in a census. Joseph gets a donkey for Mary to ride because her baby is almost ready to be born.

While Mary and Joseph are in Bethlehem, Jesus is born in a stable, because there is no room for them in the inn.

Mary welcomes many guests to the stable—the shepherds and Wise Men from the East.

Mary and Joseph take their baby to the Temple. An old man named Simeon blesses Jesus. A holy woman named Anna tells everyone that this baby is very important. Mary remembers this moment forever.

An angel tells Joseph in a dream that King Herod wants to kill the child Jesus. That night, Joseph takes Mary and Jesus to Egypt so his family will be safe.

When Jesus is a young boy, Joseph brings Mary and Jesus back to Nazareth. Their neighbors are glad to see them.

When Jesus is 12, Mary and Joseph take Him to the Temple in Jerusalem. He stays behind to ask questions of the teachers and listen to their answers. Mary and Joseph worry that they have lost their son!

We call Joseph the patron saint of a happy death. Mary and Jesus, who is now a young man, are at his bedside when he dies in his sleep.

When Jesus begins to preach and teach and people follow Him to listen, Mary often travels with Him. She likes to fix His lunch just like your mother likes to feed you.

The first miracle of Jesus is at a wedding reception in Cana. Mary tells Jesus that there is no more wine for the guests. Because Mary asks Him, Jesus turns the water into wine.

Jesus helps many people for three years, but then the leaders arrest Him and sentence Him to death. Mary rushes to be with her son as He carries His heavy cross.

Mary stands as close as the soldiers will let her while Jesus is dying. Jesus asks His apostle John to take care of Mary. He asks Mary to be a mother to John and to all of us.

Very sad, Mary goes with John and some of Jesus' disciples to lay the body of Jesus in a cave-like tomb.

On Sunday, when Mary Magdalene comes back to the tomb with other women who love Jesus, an angel tells them that Jesus is not there. He is alive! They rush to tell Mary and the Apostles.

On Pentecost, Mary and the Apostles receive the Holy Spirit. God gives them His wisdom and power to share the story of Jesus with people everywhere.

Mary lives a long time after Jesus goes back to heaven. She teaches the Apostle John many things about her son Jesus.

When Mary dies, she is taken right up to heaven because she is so good, so full of courage and love.

God the Father crowns Mary as the Queen of Heaven and Earth.
Dear Mother Mary, pray for us, now and at the hour of our death.
Amen.